THE
BEATITUDES
of
∾ EKATERINA ∿

OTHER BOOKS BY RICHARD JARRETTE

Beso the Donkey

A Hundred Million Years of Nectar Dances

THE
BEATITUDES
of
~ EKATERINA ~

poems

Richard Jarrette

GREEN WRITERS PRESS   *Brattleboro, Vermont*

Printed in the United States

10 9 8 7 6 5 4 3 2 1

Green Writers Press is a Vermont-based publisher whose mission is to spread a message of hope and renewal through the words and images we publish. Throughout we will adhere to our commitment to preserving and protecting the natural resources of the earth. To that end, a percentage of our proceeds will be donated to environmental activist groups. Green Writers Press gratefully acknowledges support from individual donors, friends, and readers to help support the environment and our publishing initiative.

GReen
wRiTers
press

Giving Voice to Writers Who Will Make the World a Better Place
Green Writers Press | Brattleboro, Vermont
www.greenwriterspress.com

ISBN: 978-0998701264

COVER BACKGROUND IMAGE:
CATHERINE CAULFIELD RUSSEL, *Snow Shadows*, oil on canvas
COVER FOREGROUND IMAGE:
ALBERTO GIACOMETTI. *Large Standing Woman II & Large Standing Woman III*
from the Donald M. Kendall Sculpture Gardens

PRINTED ON PAPER WITH PULP THAT COMES FROM FSC-CERTIFIED FORESTS, MANAGED FORESTS THAT GUARANTEE RESPONSIBLE ENVIRONMENTAL, SOCIAL, AND ECONOMIC PRACTICES BY LIGHTNING. SOURCE ALL WOOD PRODUCT COMPONENTS USED IN BLACK & WHITE, STANDARD COLOR, OR SELECT COLOR PAPERBACK BOOKS, UTILIZING EITHER CREAM OR WHITE BOOKBLOCK PAPER, THAT ARE MANUFACTURED IN THE LAVERGNE, TENNESSEE PRODUCTION CENTER ARE SUSTAINABLE FORESTRY INITIATIVE® (SFI®) CERTIFIED SOURCING.

No, tsarevitch, I am not the one
You want me to be.
And no longer do my lips
Kiss—they prophesy.

—ANNA AKHMATOVA

Contents

❧

I.

II.

III.

IV.

V.

VI.

IV

THE
BEATITUDES
of
EKATERINA

From This Shore

And I'm still here at the other end
Of this long, long wave, listening.
                              —Joy Harjo

Death used to take care of death
now we heap the plate with everything there is
no rules about it anywhere.

Spring six weeks early again birds too soon,
too late, my ears found by dizzy
worker bees, lone migrant.

Singers open-throated as skylarks, voices
uplifted with the wolves, beseech
the stars against ruin.

Your dead-silence panicked my fiery horses.
I send a breath just further with my flute
Ekaterina, does it go all the way?

I.

One Hair Of An Honest Dog

Raucous crows drive off buzzards
near the clouds.

Woodpeckers hammer oak and water tower
confer on the telephone pole cross.

What do I cleave to?

I drift to my book and find a wisp on the page.
Earth and wind gave this to me,

today's manna—

token of a ripe muse, Shakespeare's
Dark Lady, or one hair

of an honest dog.

You Stayed Away So Long

A gopher snake fat as my wrist poured out of its rock
wall to sunlight between rose and rosemary

like a Socrates *come from somewhere else*
bearing disturbing news. My kindred mind slides

toward coils so that all day on errands—the mail
good buys on wine and bosc pears—I question the air.

Emily Dickinson boarded the gondola of her silver
fairy moon heading to Baltimore but you Katya

stepped out onto our world an *aborigine of the sky*
in our time amused by *reveries* and *bachelor cigars*.

You hear the music before it arrives, said Neil Young.
I'd been in Argentina burning our tangos.

Complex Knots

A woman defining the perfect black dress,
bored with her fool's soliloquy, performs

slow-motion sambas with a smooth shoulder—
the eye of her tight strawberry blonde bun

reading my mind at the bar—loosens complex
knots she's made of her phthalo green scarf.

Ekaterina

What could be more satisfying than a hero's welcome
for bringing down the junta with a poem?

In the meantime a woman
wearing less than a yard of silk
approaches.

Birds sing.

I'm flowing with cloud names—*cumulus, cirrus*
uncinus, noctilucent.

I lift my cup, forgiving debts.

Blue Nora

A street musician on resophonic mandolin
painted her face baby blue, gothic
black eyeliner, blood-red lips.

Thirteen pomegranate seed buttons descend
throat to waist—*I wonder who gets to open those?*

The one who kisses her grandmother's hand.
I'll write it down for you
(Akhmatova's tongue).

Where does your grandmother live?
In the ground in Vsevolozhsk near St. Petersburg.
I'll kiss her sepulchre in the snow.

It's Been A Good Year

A young physicist said I must learn to act like light.

I'm taken for Jack Nicholson three times—
this afternoon while drinking a beer
in a sunny spot at my favorite café—

and I met Ekaterina
who likes to order a whole fish
and eat the eyes.

Last night she reached into a bowl of turkey parts
set aside for the cat and seized the heart.

HOLY

Clouds of dust and leaves swirl in the headlights.
After too much saké we drive with imagined cool

to the billiard lounge rowing over small waves.
13th century choral love songs from the Montpellier

Codex fill the car with such purity that silence
seems to have found the voice abreast of silence.

Blood Salt

Pain has found work—

we sleep skin to skin
warm valleys to hills

deep rivers.

Blind waves find the colors and music
they were meant for

lift our lingering salt
and light.

Our Cirque du Soleil

I believed if I held you close
you would be here in the morning.

I poured red wine over a white goat for Aphrodite,
you posed a one-hand handstand for an hour—

kind smile—the world turning
on your palm.

EVERYONE SAT DOWN

One step onto the dance floor
carved your name in it.

Five-two, maybe, my Everest—
blue oxygen required.

II.

Love's Illusions

When earth takes back the spring and summer of the trees
we do not accuse the liquid amber of being insincere.

We might reflect, ponder death, or the Dog Star—
yet another fire that does not know its name.

The Lucent Text

Our port hovered between Pacific mist and looming
clouds conceding a glimpse of arctic blue sky.

We half-guess navigated by sound to a sea lion haul out
slipping by dreams and groans to white yarrow

on the headland above. *Skylarks are a delicacy in Japan,*
you murmured, *people pray for the invitation to feast—*

the lucent text on your face fragments of my Sappho—
] *listen into* [ ] *sweetclover* [ ] *my ankles*

WHY I DROVE SIX HOURS THE NEXT DAY WITH PEARLS

The night we met you looked beyond my left eye and stammered,
On the cobblestones-to the fountain-around the corner-
follow my shadow—no corner no cobblestones

no fountain—and slithered into your Mercedes Benz
convertible for Los Angeles, Russian choir intoning *Psalms*.
I was captured by your otherworld nature

as if here the resurrection you died to and hadn't quite
worked it out like Chaplin's Little Tramp spilling
his charts to the wind mid-ocean;

sighs of a gnostic liturgy in Samuel Beckett's dream; the eerie
pins of being recalled—mate of long voyage to the harbors
of your Ithakas dragooned by Phoenician perfumes.

Our Paradiso

Our feet were on the ground with the right number of toes
and we had grave expressions tender as figures
in a Giotto painting—human, Deo volente.

Friends saw a Giacometti woman and a dog of hunger and threat—
we saw Hieronymus Bosch devils heating pokers,
rolling out the Catherine Wheels.

The living Mona Lisa raged at Leonardo in her rooms,
I carried a rose in my teeth and honed the knives—
one weapon against a world gone wrong.

God played dice against us, Einstein, in his fucking Vegas.
The crossbow—wood of the yew and oxen shoulder muscle
joined by glue from roofs of the mouths of Caspian

Sea sturgeon—the dire weapon for five hundred years.
We held together with our tangos and shared cat
drawn with *the sun and the other stars.*

WHO AGAINST THE BLIND STREAM HAVE MADE
YOUR ESCAPE FROM THE ETERNAL PRISON?

Prettiest pauses her recitativo, *I love Dante*
despite the vulgarity of his dialect—deadpan.

Dogs are reliable—St. Petersburg to Mendocino—
they know me and the vulgarity of Dante's dialect.

All the way down in my battle with the tangled clouds
I made peace with the vulgarity of Dante's dialect.

Heart-soothing eyes lift—*Che siete voi che contro*
al cieco fiume fuggita avete la pregione eternna?

The wine dark sea, far lone sail, white pelican—
Katya smiles at *the vulgarity of Dante's dialect.*

God-weather

We played in Nebuchadnezzar's killing furnace with abandon—
our God-weather mild enough, smooth sailing most

of the time—you cuddling with the king's lions me throwing bones
with the executioners, a few herby beers some laughs.

But God-weather's shifty—drove me drinking the black inkwell
straight down and you sewing up the runic epitaph carved

into your thighs with the clean instruments in your closet.
Our love talk blew all over the place in the goddamn weather—

I lick the honey of your poems from God-fingers, you purred.
A fragment of you solves the fractal equation of God-beauty, said I.

Like Giacometti drawing the death portrait of Georges Braque—
Wake up—you cannot be dead Katya. You are not dead.

WAKE—MY ANNA AKHMATOVA

Above the passion fruit vine overspilling the boundary fence
a cabbage white madly white whips ten thousand boats
to the west with her pale green fans.

The morning clouds have become this one butterfly and the silence
I've kept these five days with memories of our divina commedia.

Palms of prisoners and the wings of exhausted angels
beat against the blind walls of Stalin's castle.

Requiem—My Virginia Woolf

I didn't know the contours of my own face
until you held it in your hands and said,
I'm taking this everywhere.

These seven days seem like seven thousand years
since you walked into your River Ouse
laden with one moment more.

I think the tip of your cigar held aloft the last
thing you saw laughter forcing black
water into your lungs.

Here west wind gnarls a cypress on the headland
fragments of what I can release of you swirl
through sea grass on the tide.

My Nausicaä

I loved feeding dinner to you in the bathtub fork
by fork as you lathered and sponged—
no shame on your eyelids.

Wasn't Death surprised when like a jaguar in her season
you desired him and shyness lowered
his eyes sparing many?

Pondering Fragment 88b of Sappho
] *whatever you*] *I shall love*
On The Anniversary Of Your Death

Hike past rattlesnakes to abandoned house we found
at the edge of wilderness—caved roof three

walls empty doorframe skew-jawed to wind still ghostly—
stir the leaves we laid down our bed in.

Happiness did not concern us, you said, '*our wings
had not been made for there*'—citing

the *Paradiso* of your Dante, a shrug for the irony.
Nothing ever escaped you but smoke.

The Katya of Euripides

Birds—progeny of meadowlarks that sweetened
our day as you brushed Coco the Cat in the sun.

Cottonwoods—wild as once wild for us beyond
the leaded glass of our bedroom window.

Bible upside down on bookshelf—Artemis
calls for hounds and the silver New Moon bow.

I'm ninety three million miles from harbor
splayed on the battlefield by ten thirsty swords.

The bells of St. Mark's toll the second hour third
hour—surely the real Katya abides in Egypt.

III.

SUITE: BLESSED THE KRAFTGÄNGE

There is something maddeningly attractive
about the untranslatable, about a word
that goes silent in transit.
—ANNE CARSON

Ekaterina.

I try the hand in my left glove the right
the head under my hat—

arms open face lifts to the sky trees lose their tongues
to wind mountains cease proclaiming *massif*
become undulating river valleys seafloor—

something always torn away something always
arriving before the nails of language no
vault of heaven no *beginning.*

. . . .

You couldn't reach me in your dream of fog
though muscles and tendons
strained and tore—

the interference of demons suspected.
But your fog and your demons
found me.

· · · · · · ·

At a confluence of awarenesses obscured
by churning I study your first letter,
employ principles of philology:

She gathered up the all fragments,
But couldn't make them fit.
АННА АХМАТОВА

A warning:

Hurled to earth—
] fallen [ ] catastrophe sea [ ] panic-men [
Paradiso to Inferno getting smaller.

My neck twists in wonder at your Akhmatova—
Vita Nuova of Dante by heart?—the half-grin at your
Sappho's *glukupikros-sweetbitter* coffee.

· · · · · · ·

You settle debts and make arrangements
for Africa, the unsayable to come,
breathe a Russian phrase—

Na ryekakh vavilonskikh
tamo syedokhom
i plakakhom.

*(By the rivers of Babylon
 there we sat and wept).*

*The most anguished lament
of the Orthodox psalter,*
you say. *Alliluia.*

. . . .

I'm overswept by memories of spring harvest below our yard to the west, swallows nesting in eaves above our entry door. *How can we live under one roof on Main Street? Kill the ceiling,* you purred, *the roof will follow—then Freud.* I lost my nerve stepped backward off the edge of our green world without a butterfly or Coco the Cat, you to Nigeria with Médecins Sans Frontières—wars and horrors, kidnapped-unpersoned-ransomed—and in a reverie en route home after the terrors grinned and cracked, *A five hour layover in Newark New Jersey is worse.*

I knew your mind and the feelings without language nor wires for muscles to give them familiar colors. *Love is a single soul inhabiting two bodies,* Aristotle said, but you were one of those fey beings scarce arrived as Sappho without the missing volumes and lyre. I think we were one and a half people and my self of you half-aware of some far fragrant and clouded world.

I sense with your legs and peer through eyes tracking women dragged from gurneys—from surgery, childbirth, ectopic pregnancy—tortured and killed in the dirt by fundamentalists, you volunteers forced to watch and watch unblinking—*too late maybe after now*—and you run to the *now* where she bleeds out as those men shake their knives, shoot the sky, and praise God.

35

．． ． ． ．． ．

Canary Island Pines sway on the high air
junipers unmoved the stand of laurels thrilled.

All our days uplifted by trees through their seasons
a burnt offering to the silence-seeing stars.

Birds open unhinged doors to the wild
my wings drag on the dusty ground—still

this rasping upward seeking voice more earthly—
Nearer my leaves to thee.

． ． ． ． ．． ．

My reveries soften with arrival of winter rains
in your second death year—

Earth's face always open my heart
not turned away.

Mi corazón, como una sierpe,
se ha desprendido de su piel,
y acquí la miro entre mis dedos,
llena de heridas y de miel.

(Like a snake, my heart
has shed its skin.
I hold it there in my hand,
full of honey and wounds.)
—Federico García Lorca

. . . .

Desire sings of a heart not bereft—
released one, far past returning, ashes of the chambers of your salty
mortal muscle—the Paris of your joys our starry nights
in a glance, murmurs of wrist and neck little ear
chiming, your body the lip of one heart
mine the other.

. . . .

Tormented-seeming clouds throw a sword of light
to a mountain that accepts.

. . . .

You flew on a west wind toward the Sierra I could not
hold your thin smoke in my arms close to my chest.

A dream-voice said, *Run into the woods.*
My dream-thought, *You there in a glade*

poised on your one-hand handstand—strange
little tree—Coco the Cat near.

. . . .

Massive silence, cathedral bell missing its iron tongue
struck by phantoms—hours without tolls

to answer, the glance from labors, moan from sleep—
the silence of eternity too soon.

. . . .

Late December leaves blanket the yard
gather in a pile at my door yellows and browns.

The season for dying into earth arrives—passage
toward roots and rebirth—as above so below.

What I cleave to our hands unclasp at a whisper—
Blessed the Kraftgänge who are the flowing

and the channel in which it flows.

. . . .

The night more day
a world overthrown by moon

figures pale in silver air
deer unsure

the empire of mind
some mist.

BLESSED ARE THOSE WHO GATHER

Guttering cries escape our plundered hearts at the Requiem.

Pulsing murmurations of starlings on the shadow-breathing air—
visual perfume, silent *Benedictus*, sky's corps de ballet—

Blessed are those who gather.

Grasped by the twelve-fingered fisherman passing the *Peace*
hooks of faith and miracle set in my jaws—fantastic nests appear below
the Dragon Trees of Madagascar eight-foot crows among the Wine Palms.

The Celebrant offers comfort—*Do you know there's not a word for 'trespass'*
in Finland nor in the Kingdom of Heaven?

I remember your kindness—that poor woman with the appalling
edema who sat at her labors in the laundromat struggling
for breath—you touched the elephantine legs,

fussed with the mad hair she laughing, conjured jubilating
songbirds from the slack mouth. In the car you said,

A lost Stradivarius I gave her my red lipstick.

BLESSED ARE THE POLYTONAL

Only you my sweet catastrophe could see under my hat—
Human forms are puny desire is vast and absolute

shot through with the composition logic of Arnold Schönberg
who berated definitions in his democracy of tones.

Am I not your donkey which you have ridden all your life to this day?
You were so proud of my turn as Balaam's Ass. *Aphrodite I am,*

you said, *blessed are the polytonal the unafraid of a possible truth,*
your little grin at my violent nightmares unnerving but lovely.

Love me, love my umbrella—how you relished your *Giacomo Joyce*—
gathered hundreds of exotic paper cocktail favors left them

in odd places, fractal patterns slipped between the piano keys
mapping a troubled Webern chord—courteous warning

when overtaken by perilous desires—or puzzled out a surreal
phrase of Satie gaiety when the skin had a happy day.

I open one of your tiny crêpe umbrellas under night sky Venus
kissing crescent moon it seems and dance the sad clown

lamenting our Fred & Ginger of the studio smooth as polished
ebony, silk underthings, wild for Ornette Coleman's *Song X.*

Blessed Whose Silence Overspills

A whirlwind wrapped in poplar leaves rose up from my street
slim-waisted en pointe and revealed—

Blessed whose silence overspills you are the conjuring bowl.

I entered the whirling open-armed steadied by raven and mourning dove
skinned of my battle gear blind as a moonless blood river—

your hands telling me that I was secure and the glorious trumpet
of the ascended Elijah praising and there were horses.

Suite: Blessed Who Are The Sacrifice

Akhmatova—the name is a vast sigh
and it falls into depths without name.
                                    —Marina Tsvetayeva

The night and the stars of Akhmatova's ardor
reach through the photograph.

It seemed to me that stormclouds with stormclouds
Collided somewhere on high
And a flying flash of lightning
And a voice of great joy
Descended like angels upon me.

Our third day, you're wearing nothing
but my hand painted tie.

. . . .

On my knees I find the grim-faced pawn lost under our bed—
I loved those flowery battles with your lipstick draftee
fierce for your haunted tongue.

A guest approaches on horseback along the golden grain.
The steady, certain, ring of his spurs.
He kisses my Grandmother's hand in the drawing room
And my lips on the curving staircase.

—*Lovely,* I say.
—*It's about death,* you say.

. . . .

No food, Tsvetayeva places her daughter in an orphanage
where she dies of starvation.

People like Job in this world who might
even have envied him. If.

Marina takes her life, Anna Andreyevna carries
the poem until it disintegrates.

. . . .

Mayakovsky—roughneck—Vladimir V
can't pass by God without threatening him with a jackknife,
reads nothing but Akhmatova days in love
yet wants her purged—*Writes of Angels!*
At the last his suicide poem kind.

As they say, incident dissolved.
Love's boat smashed against existence.

. . . .

Anna tears the bones from her body to appease Stalin—
burns her poems burns her angels and the moonlight on the gillyflowers,
composes Soviet verse glorifying *him whose fingers are worms,*
mind in hell flames—to save her son, Lev.

. . . .

I've become thready as a painting of some age you can hold to the light
and see the Belgian linen unraveling, the other side bleeding
through warps and woofs.

Not one feathered word, Katya, not one to reach you *Little Sparrow.*
The gold dime under my tongue buys nothing but shame.

I don't know who cut a window
into the tomb, Anna Akhmatova says.

. . . .

(*Chorus*)

And it drips in sleep before my heart
the grief-remembering pain.
We learn unwillingly.
From the high bench of the gods
by violence, it seems, grace comes.

—AESCHYLUS, *Agamemnon*

. . . .

Old pine backlit by a passing car—
shiver of my flensed soul in the light
that went with you.

Sun and moon illumine heart-shaped bindweed flowers
snaking down a ditch
by the road,

perennial roots fifteen feet below the surface
almost unfailing
spring and summer.

You flung your beautiful at eternity.

Blessed Are Those Who Release

Divine the über-goodness that makes us
make angels in the snow.

Released in Oregon this morning, a rescued Bald Eagle
lifted itself on wings fluid as a manta ray of the sky,
joyful applause from kind distance.

Late February, vernal equinox a month away, sunlit birds—
notes of resurrection through wispy
birch-hair nerves of winter.

They say you returned to the angels when you released
yourself, Ekaterina, that you're comforting
casualties in Nigeria. *Triage*, I say.

IV.

Replies to Ch'ü Yüan (340-278 B.C.E.)
The Question of Heaven

Answers do not matter so much as questions, said the Good Fairy. A good question is very hard to answer. The better the question the harder the answer. There is no answer at all to a very good question.

—FLANN O'BRIEN, *At Swim-Two-Birds*

Wool Socks

Eating onions and potatoes
feeling less unsolved—

memories of skating in the house,
childlike gaiety in our socks.

I leave my shoes and lie on the grass
in mild weather, listen to the big

animal down there grumbling—
the one that's pulled my tail

fifty million years so far
keeping me close to the ground.

Clouds lit by fiery dragons and chariots,
a single drop of rain

falling through a loon's
night passage cry

onto the back of a sheep
in the pasture.

From the far origin of all antiquity
who hands the story down to us?

THE LAWS AND THE PROPHECIES

My neighbor's jasmine pours over the fence
and keeps good company by the kitchen window
open warm nights to invite the airy fragrance

to my pillow. I remember when you scented my floral sheets
with your perfume Katya, a journey mapped by Dante—
books tossed aside, shoes, and we erased

the commandments written on our embezzled skins
and made the laws and the prophecies
to guide our forever.

Before heaven and earth take shape,
how do you delve into what's there?

THE PRIMAL OBSTRUCTION

I believe in birds and the lucent songs stars burn themselves
to death for, and thee—I won't be late though the way obscured.

Yellow-rumped warblers forage seeds among the courtyard bricks
of St. Mark's, the choir director has gathered the children
hearthside for sleigh bell shaking practice—

stragglers skip by unaware they've startled birds into a magnolia close
on the church where prayers rise with candle smoke for spirit
touched leaders who might abandon disgraceful wars.

And I worry about the teacher losing a black spike heel
to the cracks, taking a fall—*I could catch you in my arms, hopes
harmonizing in our eyes, shepherds piping.*

Mated crows share the meat of one walnut cleft by a toss
from the copper rain gutter. My horoscope encourages today
claims I have something like the *bucket wheel excavator*

in my tool box—largest machine in the world—blade four stories
tall for cutting through mountains in Kazakhstan. *It's time
Taurus to overcome the primal obstruction.*

Navigation-chirps hold the warbler flock together for trilling
in the high branches, a waxing moon drifts over the river valley—
sky flung wide open mountain to mountain.

> *When light and dark are still a blur,
> who can see through to their source?*

Late Winter

If knowing requires an entire body I have a hundred
ninety pounds of it a god awful waste—

the old drunk Chinese poets laugh at me I'm older
than most of them ever were and

wine—aswim through pictures painted on the window
into the loam of things anchor chain cut.

When it's altogether primal chaos,
how do you see the shape of things?

OLD MAN SHOVELING SNOW

I shovel drifting snow to lock the chicken coop gate
against raccoons and weasels, more dumps on my neck

when I lift the laden cedar boughs in its swing path—
cold shock awakens memory of *church-steeple-people*

on my mother's torn lap when I was three years old
yesterday afternoon in the City of Angels.

Blazing radiance and utter darkness
and nothing more: how did it happen?

Reverie—Jackson's Island

Looking east for the Spring Moon I do believe
it shows Missouri—the muddy Mississippi
River slides through my soul.

Your *Purgatorio*, Katya—my *Jackson's Island*,
Huckleberry Finn chews on his death
with a smoke between shores.

The sky looks ever so deep when you lay down
on your back in the moonshine.

The serious old water tells wide his sanctuary—
canoe hidden in the low hanging willows
a confidence secure with the snakes.

I hear Lao Tzu's banjo—
Flourish at the wildest edges of it all
sustained by a quiet heart.

Huck abides with summer berries and catfish,
fire, counting drift logs then the stars.
And so for three days and nights.

And when yin and yang first gave birth—
what was rooted, and what transformed?

Of Our All

The black granite under my boots looms
at fourteen thousand feet a few miles west.

Neck bends a finger unfurls it wants to draw the line
from Bering Strait to Straits of Magellan.

A good rock in hand found on the mule deer path
glitters with its own stars and galaxies

each an echo of the firmament and a dogged moon—
rebirth portent of our all again?

Nine celestial compass points arrayed,
calibrated perfectly, and measured out
just so—how was heaven ever made,
how, in the beginning, set in motion?

I Hear You Laughing As The Hens Cackle At First Light

Snow falling on the divide light on the high prairie.
Rocky Mountain dwarf junipers razor blue

reach an inch and a half toward the sun this lifetime.
The morning star gleams in dewdrop and meadowlark's eye—

heavens tethered by a descending
whistle and chickens.

How could its vast turning be tethered?

Volant Heart

Relics of old forest circle the grassy hilltop
and a vulture standing there who bows northeast

spreads the dry wings and rises on a spiraling air
without apparent effort lifted by your eyebrow.

And how is its axle-pole lifted there?

The Buddha, Katya

Crown to toes the bronze body weeps
right hand runneth over

with spring rain and my lamentations—
creeksong in the cottonwoods after hushed years.

Grass Mountain uplifts grass
and the blue lupine.

How were its eight pillars put in place?

The Last Poem Before A Thousand Years Of Peace

What inspires? asks Ekaterina just now it seems—*could be
anything,* I say, *handful of gravel*—mixed forest

on the mountain hisses clouds close—*you ever near
silence after the hawk screams the liminal roar.*

Numberless voices cross your threshold keening—*cries
of the lost migrants and refugees the wind cut wires—*

the world is the disfigured women writhing at your feet
and we're forced to choose, working out the triage.

Thelonious Sphere Monk lays down a nest of chords
for the demons of his angels, Nina Simone sings *freedom.*

And why is the southeast tilting down?

Hiking Into A Cloud

I caught a glimpse of you in the mountains with Han Shan
or my phantoms below cliffs hung with green mosses—

rain hats and walking sticks hopping stone to stone
crossing a stream—I'll have to get reliably lost to catch up.

The boundaries of its nine regions—
how could they join, how lead away?

Two Marys

I love the way you said, *There should be two Marys—*
the Virgin, and the other one with her infinite promise

and, *I can go there.* But that page we couldn't quite hold
down long enough our psycho-historical demons busy.

O mournful bedtimes—your odd comfort with nightmares,
the hot humid countries you called them, and the winds

ever too fierce for other stars and other god, the happy one.
I loved coming home to contortion practice your single-

piece python-pattern leotard Coco the Cat ignoring *whatever—*
riderless black horses in the kitchen dust devils in the dojo.

If not Schönberg we turned ourselves on Lizst's spiritual lathe—
Bénédiction de Dieu dans la solitude, Pensées des morts.

I love how you tore through my closet saying, *You never wear*
this or this, you're never going to lose enough weight for that,

and took half my things to the hospital for the homeless who
haunted and scavenged out there in the night. How tender

quiet mornings with *glukupikros* coffee eyes deep the little
grin regaling me with shanghais of your most lost souls

gathered in for bath-food-thorough physical-delousing-
manicure-pedicure-haircut-new clothes-vitamins-bottles

of water-a bit of cash. *And then they look like farolitos—
luminarias—drifting off on the river of shadows,* you said.

*And all their meanders back and forth,
who knows how many there might be?*

READING LI PO

War after war mothers find the guts of children
dropped by crows strung on the dead trees.

Monks immolate themselves at prayer for peace
brew the kerosene and diesel strike the match.

I'm standing here Ekaterina—yet, for what?
You danced swing the night of our confluence

whispered, *I love Dante, trauma medicine, fractals,*
and pulled my poor bones onto the dance floor.

Couples share stories of finding themselves
together—the ridiculous accidents of fate—

reveal more than they know sometimes trade
that lit glance which says, *Now this too.*

The longer you survived Death's unbroken gaze
in the wars the more unbroken here.

What makes heaven entire and whole?

Star Dust

The river that took you is larger than the river.
There's no thinking it through.

And how is it split into twelve palaces?

VISIONS OF EKATERINA

Tu Mu asks,

Who can manage such distances of the heart?

The patio table joined by one thread of spider silk
to a branch of autumn sage,

southern Mexico to central California
by a hummingbird's tongue in the white blossom.

Li Po becomes the moon with wine.

That tango under our first moon caught us
in a web of sorrow and desire

like Rilke's dog with a thorn in his paw—
And everywhere he goes he is no longer a dog,

but rather a thorn, something he does not
understand and that cannot be understood.

It was you who opened your pores to listen—
and Coco his eyes on your lap—

when I said, *The volume of a gnat's blood*
is equal to the Sea of Tranquillity.

How were sun and moon joined together?

The Center

Starlight in the dead eye of a poor goldfinch,
tendrils of Milky Way unfurl in a wheeling dot—

do your hips turn its turning at that tango dance hall
on the other side of the Swan, Katya?

Winds and Pacific tides churn your scatters.
I find you in the empty drifting eye of a storm.

And how are scattered stars patterned?

Legacy

The dawn sun finds you in my eyes
where you stir night under the lids.

Here's the world again just as it is—
wars, rosemary, red-winged blackbird.

I asked the President and Joint Chiefs
to spare the powerless as you wished.

The pepper tree waves shaggy branches
on light airs this mild May morning.

Rising from the depths of Boiling Abyss,
returning to rest in the Gulf of Obscurity,
from morning light on to evening dark;
the sun's journey lasts how many miles?

FOREVER BORN

Prettiest Girl, laughing, amused
eyebrow—nesting doves.

I write a letter to our first-kiss moon
in the east and to the last.

Dear mother of silk and assassins,
of love and Kali—the soft-deadly
edges of your sword.

Mercy.

Then night's radiant one—by what power
can it die out and soon come back to life,
a bright moon?

On Shakespeare's Sonnet 17

In the dream I'm offered half a chicken
to feed my dog
and overcharged for it.

I don't have a dog.

I order wine
though I swore it off
last night.

It means my love poems fail
no matter how many christians
I sacrifice—

the first word
seals Shakespeare's *tomb,*
hides your life.

The desperados trouble
Aristotle's dust
who said,

Euripides was the most tragic
of the tragedians.

Full moon at midday—
romance waiting to happen—
O earthly faces.

And what does it gain from a rabbit
inside its belly gazing out?

CERTAINTY

Survivors lean in to you for the portrait,
laugh with skewed mouths repaired
after torture and mutilation.

Your sweaty face shines makeup
not possible yet eyebrows shaped
for endless amusement—

smiled as you plucked, smiled
as you cut your thighs
with scalpel, smiled and stitched
before we'd go dancing.

I ponder your request to just once
trace scars with my fingertip
as you translated.

The hysterectomy—so young,
dead certain—made way for the glad
sisters in the photograph.

Star Mother never mated—so how is it
she gave birth to nine star-children?

More Elusive Than The Great White Whale

The floor of our house seemed to slant south Monday, northeast
by Friday, or southwest—where does great Elder Wind-Star live?

You laughed when a king snake slithered in—I stabbed shadows
with a stick—was that great Elder Wind-Star in its obsidian eye?

It was always 3 A.M.—the clocks lied—we asked Coco the Cat
to explain because wasn't he in on it with great Elder Wind-Star?

The puzzled marriage, tricky equation—making love was like
dissecting a frog—where was great Elder Wind-Star to guide us?

We followed a ravine to the sea—cargo ships heading west
with our dusk—surely the great Elder Wind-Star just beyond?

Unsure, amused, the muddy climb up appeared far too steep
but wouldn't great Elder Wind-Star be there? Seals barked.

We jumped over the cosmos in a puddle holding hands searching
for great Elder Wind-Star—an answer superior to the question?

Where does great Elder Wind-Star live?

Is There Refuge Also In The Merciless?

The seething firmament harrows my bones—
maybe the dreams of the dead are this life,
slender accident, fleeting grail.

I feel the sun and the wind on your eyes
as you brush your long hair above the fields
taking in the liquors of the day.

Yes you turned to the black wall
passed through on the thirtieth of July
to your seven night sisters the Pleiades.

*I venture no more than a low whisper, afraid
I'll wake the people of heaven,* said Li Po.

And where do warm ch'i breezes dwell?

LITTLE SPARROW

Hopping around my shoe, cockeyed closer look
at my fingers, you don't seem to fear me.

Did the winds of eternity lift your wings today?
Grass Mountain already one grain of salt.

What closes in to bring evening dark?

What Brings

The wonder with which you touched snow after Nigeria.

Our one moment on religion you said, *The blind beggar*
on the church porch cold mornings in the Machado poem—

Más vieja que la iglesia tiene alma. I loved your gift for waking
languages with your tongue and with your eyes and sometimes

with your hips and breasts—*He has a soul older than the church.*
And then you took Coco's face in your hands, careful

with the whiskers—*He has seen las blancas sombras de las horas*
santas, the white shadows of the holy hours.

The cat slipped away, your eyes followed to his lookout above
the fields and the long light, killdeer, and plowing.

The reverence with which you touched snow before dying.

What opens out to bring morning light?

Spirits Of Katya

Winters meander—grief can't quite rot into earth—
trembling peach blossoms appear late January.

A spring fire took eight thousand acres of salt bush,
mountain lilac, and lemons—the sanguine spirits

of death climb perennial roots earlier each year.
Nectars of your fragments deepen the wine.

Before the stars announcing spring rise,
how is Splendor-Spirit sun hidden away?

V.

As If In Ancient China

I linger in the night
crushing frozen grass as I stray.

Did you tie this moon to the foot of a goose
and hope to find me?

STORM

Gusts shiver the house
doors slam open
trees crack.

Morning—
face down in mud
the gate.

LESS

Ghost-quiet

yet the mass and weight of an object
moving at the speed of light.

Shy, endangered, the angel with one
shoulder everything leans on—

unsinks the ship, unkills the child, looms
behind the veils of paradox.

HAPPINESS

Abandoned house roofless three walls
no floor a ruin if you think *house*—

to brown towhees a place to scratch
in the leaves for bugs and worms,

for the male to sing a territorial song
from what remains of the chimney—

an imagination problem like the time
friends said we must be very happy

in the beautiful house we built because
they couldn't see the ruins inside us.

Piedras Blancas

Motel shuttered—
godforsaken—
vanished joy.

The shore road bears
a black heavy
Cadillac.

WINTERING

Chance
mark

on white
shore.

Sea—
frozen,

darks
below.

The Heavens Are Trying Many Things And Not Nearly Finished

The light of countless stars
rains on the roof—

particles, or waves, in the form of Coco
the Maine Coon Cat sleep

on my pillow.

OLD DANCERS

An elder couple journey
the flagstone path,

press the back of one hand
to their other's—

listen with the tiny hairs—
guide, innocent

of the winning
tango.

Enough

My house so small one candle
almost keeps it warm.

May my appetites be modest
satisfied by nearly enough.

THE BENCH

After sixty seven years of busyness
I prefer to be idle. No traffic light needed
at this crossing—*Yield* will do.

THE VASTY DEEPS

A worldly moon lays its silent music
on the ocean, the black key,
but I hear *Potato Head Blues*.

My soul, glowing down there
with long teeth, thrives on pressure
and Louis Armstrong.

Pilar

My Romani friend calls me *Death*
alleging that I have a serene appetite

for loss and throw shadows on the wall
when I laugh like dungeon torches.

VI.

The grip of life is as strong as the grip of death

All this time thinking the wolf outside my door
hungered to get inside and finish it off

he waited for me to join him out there
and vanish beyond the ashes of mortal calamity

beyond our tender psalms of praise
and lamentation—and further.

Through the river valleys tongues loose
we navigate by the resinous taste of the stars.

Adam had just performed the primordial act of naming, had taken the first step toward imposing on the wide-open pointless meaningless directionless dementia of the real a set of clichés that no one would ever dislodge, or want to dislodge—they are our human history, our edifices of thought, our answer to chaos. Eve's instinct was to bite this answer in half.

—ANNE CARSON, *Nay Rather*

Notes

CPAA—*The Complete Poems of Anna Akhmatova I & II* (Zephyr Press, 1990)
Judith Hemschemeyer, Translator.

CCP—*Classical Chinese Poetry* (FS&G, 2008) David Hinton, Translator.

Epigraph—CPAA I pg. 461.

From This Shore
And I'm still here—Joy Harjo, *Conflict Resolution for Holy Beings* (Norton,
2015) from *Charlie and the Baby* pg. 43.

You Stayed Away So Long
come from—Anne Carson, *Decreation* (Vintage, 2005) pg. 39.
Emily Dickinson—Anne Carson, *If Not, Winter: Fragments of Sappho*
(Vintage, 2002) pg. 371 and *Emily Dickinson Letters* (Knopf, 2011) Emily
Fragos, Editor pg. 241.

The Lucent Text
fragments—in the format of Carson's *Sappho.*

Why I Drove Six Hours The Next Day With Pearls
Ithakas—C.P. Cavafy *The Canon* (Center for Hellenic Studies, 2007) Stratis
Haviaras, Translator pg.91

Our Paradiso
crossbow—*Scientific American*, January, 1985, Palmer, Foley, Soedel.
the sun and the other stars—*W. S. Merwin Selected Translations* (Copper
Canyon, 2013) *Canto XXXIII, Paradiso,* Dante pg. 325.

Who against the blind stream have made
your escape from the eternal prison?
    Dante Alighieri, *Purgatorio* (Copper Canyon, 2013), W.S. Merwin, Translator,
    from *Canto I* pg. 5.

God-weather
    Alex Danchev, *Georges Braque* (Arcade, 2005)—Giacometti draws the death
    portrait pg. 259.

My Nausicaä
    Anne Carson, *Decreation* (2005) pg. 34—*She is the cleanest girl in epic.*
    Anne Carson, *Grief Lessons* (NYRB, 2006) pg. 311—*Shame lives on the eyelids.*

Pondering Fragment 88B of Sappho
    ] *whatever you*] *I shall love*
    On The Anniversary Of Your Death
    If Not, Winter: Fragments of Sappho (2002) Anne Carson, Translator pg. 177.
    our wings—W.S. Merwin Selected Translations (Copper Canyon, 2013) pg. 325.

The Katya Of Euripides
    Euripides, *Helen, The Complete Euripides Volume V* (Oxford, 2011), Peter
    Burian, Translator. *We are in Egypt*—pgs 265-266.

Suite: Blessed The Kraftgänge
    Kraftgänge—a word coined by Jakob Böhme (1575-1624).
    Epigraph—Anne Carson, *Nay Rather* (Sylph Editions, 2013) pg. 8.
    She gathered—CPAA from *Alisa* pg. 251.
    Fragments—format of Carson's *Sappho*
    glukupikros-sweetbitter from the Greek of Sappho.
    Mi corazón—*Collected Poems of Federico García Lorca* (FS&G, 2002, Revised)
    Christopher Mauer, Editor pg. 7.
    released one, far past returning—from the mantra of *The Heart Sutra,* version
    employed by Jane Hirshfield in *Letter to C., After* (Harper, 2006) pg 90: *Gone*
    now, released one, far past returning, freed one, suffer no more.

Blessed Are Those Who Gather
    Ekphrasis—*FLOCK: Birds on the Brink*, an exhibit of contemporary artists
    curated by Nancy Gifford at Ganna Walska Lotusland.

Blessed Are The Polytonal
    Human forms—*Grief Lessons* pg. 311.
    Am I not—Bible, Numbers 22:30
    Love me, love my umbrella—James Joyce, *Giacomo Joyce* (Viking, 1968) pg. 16.
    Song X, Pat Methany/Ornette Coleman (Geffen Records, 1986).

Blessed Whose Silence Overspills
Ekphrasis, *FLOCK: Birds on the Brink*. As above.

Suite: Blessed Who Are The Sacrifice
Epigraph—Marina Tsvetayeva, *Selected Poems* (Dutton, 1986), Elaine
    Feinstein, Translator pg. 15.
It seemed to me—CPAA *pg. 513*.
A guest approaches—CPAA pg. 525. Ekaterina's version.
People like Job—Tsvetayeva (1986) pg. 36.
Anna Andreyevna—Anna's given name was Anna Andreyevna Gorenko.
Her father asked that she take another name, alarmed that he had a
poet in the family, and she chose the name of a maternal Tartar
ancestor—Akhmatova. CPAA I pg. 1 and
CPAA II 761*n*—starvation of Tsvetayaeva's daughter.
As they say—CPAA I pg. 93.
him whose fingers are worms—I recall this as one of the lines that got Osip
Mandelstam arrested by Stalin, which eventually killed him.
I don't know who cut—CPAA pg. 517.
And it drips—Carson's Aeschylus version *Sappho* (2002) pg. 365. I've blended
her two lines with those of Peter Burian from his *Oresteia* in *The
Complete Aeschylus Volume I* (Oxford, 2011), *Strophe 3*, 205-210 pg. 51.

Replies to Ch'ü Yüan, *The Question of Heaven*, CCP pgs. 55-62. And see Eliot
    Weinberger, *Works on Paper* (NDP, 1986), *What Were the Questions?* pg 58

Old Man Shoveling Snow, etc.
    I reside at times on the eastern slope of the Rocky Mountains.

Reverie—Jackson's Island
    The sky—*And so for three days*—Mark Twain, *The Adventures of Huckleberry
    Finn* (University of California, 1985). Pg 49, pp. 55.
    Flourish—Lao Tzu 16, a version—mine—cobbled from Sam Hamill's *Tao Te
    Ching* (Shambhala, 2005) and David Hinton's (Counterpoint, 2000).

Reading Li Po
    Monks immolate themselves—homage to Thich Quang Duc—immolated
    himself June 11, 1963 in Saigon for peace—Tiep Hien Buddhist Order of
    Thich Nhat Hanh who composed the liturgy, *Protocol For Self Immolation:
    This is not suicide. To burn oneself by fire is to prove what one is saying is of
    utmost importance. The monk has not lost courage, nor does he, or she, desire
    non-existence, nor is this self-destruction but belief in the good fruition of this
    act of self-sacrifice for the sake of others.*

Visions of Ekaterina
Who can manage—CCP pg. 303.
And everywhere he goes—Lou Andreas-Salome, *You Alone Are Real To Me*
(BOA Editions, 2003) pg. 65.

On Shakespeare's Sonnet 17

17
Who will believe my verse in time to come
If it were filled with your most high deserts?
Though yet, heaven knows, it is but as a tomb
Which hides your life, and shows not half your parts.
If I could write the beauty of your eyes,
And in fresh numbers number all your graces,
The age to come would say, 'This poet lies;
Such heavenly touches ne'er touched earthly faces.'
So should my papers—yellowed with their age—
Be scorned, like old men of less truth than tongue,
And your true rights be termed a poet's rage
And stretched metre of an antique song:
    But were some child of yours alive that time,
    You should live twice, in it and in my rhyme.

Euripides—Anne Carson, *Grief Lessons* (2006) pg. 89: *Tragikotatos.*

Is There Refuge Also In The Merciless?
slender accident—*Hamlet*, III ii—
    Where joy most revels, grief doth most lament;
    Grief joys, joy grieves, on slender accident.
I venture no more—Li Po, CCP pg. 176.

What Brings
The blind beggar—*Times Alone: Selected Poems of Antonio Machado*
(Wesleyan, 1983) Robert Bly, Translator pg. 35.

The grip of life is as strong as the grip of death
Jane Hirshfield, *Given Sugar, Given Salt* (Harper, 2001), title from *Poem With
Two Endings* pg 55, the first ending. (The second—*but the vanished, the
vanished beloved, o where?*). Used with permission.

Epigraph
Anne Carson, *Nay Rather* (2013) pg. 26.

Acknowledgements

ॐ

I am grateful to the publications in which the following poems first appeared:

Askew
    Why I Drove Six Hours The Next Day With Pearls
    It's Been A Good Year
    Blue Nora
    Our Paradiso
    Wake—My Anna Akhmatova
The Café Review
    Requiem—My Virginia Woolf
    The Lucent Text (as Do You Remember This, Katya?)
    God-weather
Levure Littéraire 13
    The Laws And The Prophecies
    Blessed Are The Polytonal
    Who against the blind stream
Live Encounters
    Replies to Chü Yüan   *The Question of Heaven*
    Visions Of Ekaterina
    Two Marys
    Certainty
    The Last Poem Before A Thousand Years Of Peace
    More Elusive Than The Great White Whale
    What Brings

Rare Feathers: Poems On Birds And Art (Gunpowder Press, 2015)
    Blessed Are Those Who Gather
    Blessed Whose Silence Overspills
Snapdragon
    The Primal Obstruction

∾

My debt of gratitude to Jane Hirshfield is of transcendental proportions. Heartfelt thanks to Stancey Hancock who read every version so carefully. Many thanks to Sterling Price, Jim Anderson, Stephen Cline, Mary Robin Hamilton. To Dan Gerber for commenting on some of these poems, particularly Star Dust, and to Mark Russell Jones, Caleb Beissert, Gretchen Marquette, Catherine Abbey Hodges, and Mariaelena Susana Camarena, for showing me the way. All good warmth, all devotion, to Dede Cummings and her crew at Green Writers Press with a special acknowledgement of Jessica Zeng for her fine work.

CPSIA information can be obtained
at www.ICGtesting.com
Printed in the USA
LVHW01s0907031217
558378LV00004B/13/P